Look out for these  from Book House

The Danger Zone

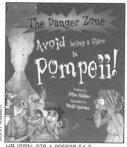
The Danger Zone
Avoid being a Slave in Pompeii!
Written by John Malam
John Malam
HB ISBN: 978-1-905638-54-3
PB ISBN: 978-1-905638-55-0

The Danger Zone
Avoid being a Victorian Servant!
Written by Fiona Macdonald
Illustrated by David Antram
Fiona Macdonald
HB ISBN: 1-904642-75-6
PB ISBN: 1-904642-76-4

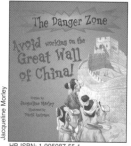
The Danger Zone
Avoid working on the Great Wall of China!
Written by Jacqueline Morley
Illustrated by David Antram
Jacqueline Morley
HB ISBN: 1-905087-55-1
PB ISBN: 1-905087-56-X

The Danger Zone
Avoid sailing with Christopher Columbus!
Written by Fiona Macdonald
Illustrated by David Antram
Fiona Macdonald
HB ISBN: 978-1-904642-11-4
PB ISBN: 978-1-904642-12-1

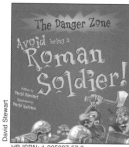
The Danger Zone
Avoid being a Roman Soldier!
Written by David Stewart
Illustrated by David Antram
David Stewart
HB ISBN: 1-905087-57-8
PB ISBN: 1-905087-58-6

The Danger Zone
Avoid being Mary, Queen of Scots!
Written by Fiona Macdonald
Illustrated by David Antram
Fiona Macdonald
HB ISBN: 978-1-905638-79-6
PB ISBN: 978-1-905638-80-2

The Danger Zone
Avoid being a wartime Evacuee!
Simon Smith
HB ISBN: 1-904194-81-8
PB ISBN: 1-904194-82-6

The Danger Zone
Avoid becoming a Pirates' Prisoner!
Written by John Malam
Illustrated by David Antram
John Malam
HB ISBN: 1-904194-18-4
PB ISBN: 1-904194-19-2

The Danger Zone
Avoid sailing on the Titanic!
Written by David Stewart
Illustrated by David Antram
David Stewart
HB ISBN: 1-904194-16-8
PB ISBN: 1-904194-17-6

The Danger Zone
Avoid sailing on a 19th-century Whaling Ship!
Written by Peter Cook
Illustrated by David Antram
Peter Cook
HB ISBN: 1-904642-13-6
PB ISBN: 1-904642-14-4

The Danger Zone
Avoid being in a Medieval Castle!
Written by Jacqueline Morley
Illustrated by David Antram
Jacqueline Morley
HB ISBN: 978-1-906370-25-1
PB ISBN: 978-1-906370-26-8

The Danger Zone
Avoid being on Apollo 13!
Written by Ian Graham
Illustrated by David Antram
Ian Graham
HB ISBN: 1-904194-55-9
PB ISBN: 1-904194-56-7

The Danger Zone
Avoid becoming an Egyptian Pyramid Builder!
Written by Jacqueline Morley
Illustrated by David Antram
Jacqueline Morley
HB ISBN: 1-904642-01-2
PB ISBN: 1-904642-02-0

The Danger Zone
Avoid entering the Ancient Greek Olympics!
Written by Michael Ford
Illustrated by David Antram
Michael Ford
HB ISBN: 1-904642-05-5
PB ISBN: 1-904642-06-3

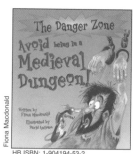
The Danger Zone
Avoid being in a Medieval Dungeon!
Written by Fiona Macdonald
Illustrated by David Antram
Fiona Macdonald
HB ISBN: 1-904194-53-2
PB ISBN: 1-904194-54-0

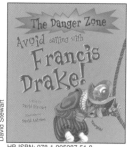
The Danger Zone
Avoid sailing with Francis Drake!
Written by David Stewart
Illustrated by David Antram
David Stewart
HB ISBN: 978-1-905087-51-8
PB ISBN: 978-1-905087-52-5

The Danger Zone
Avoid being in the Great Fire of London!
Written by Jim Pipe
Jim Pipe
HB ISBN: 978-1-906714-66-6
PB ISBN: 978-1-906714-67-3

The Danger Zone
Avoid being Tutankhamun!
Written by David Stewart
Illustrated by David Antram
David Stewart
HB ISBN: 978-1-905638-04-8
PB ISBN: 978-1-905638-05-5

The Danger Zone
Avoid meeting a Body-Snatcher!
Written by Fiona Macdonald
Illustrated by David Antram
Fiona Macdonald
HB ISBN: 978-1-906370-99-2
PB ISBN: 978-1-906714-00-0

The Danger Zone
Avoid exploring with Captain Cook!
Written by Mark Bergin
Illustrated by David Antram
Mark Bergin
HB ISBN: 978-1-905087-61-7
PB ISBN: 978-1-905087-62-4

The Danger Zone
Avoid being a Medieval Knight!
Fiona Macdonald
HB ISBN: 978-1-904642-07-7
PB ISBN: 978-1-904642-08-4

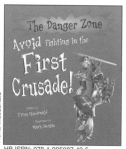
The Danger Zone
Avoid fighting in the First Crusade!
Written by Fiona Macdonald
Illustrated by Mark Bergin
Fiona Macdonald
HB ISBN: 978-1-905087-49-5
PB ISBN: 978-1-905087-50-1

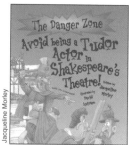
The Danger Zone
Avoid being a Tudor Actor in Shakespeare's Theatre!
Written by Jacqueline Morley
Illustrated by David Antram
Jacqueline Morley
HB ISBN: 978-1-906714-17-8
PB ISBN: 978-1-906714-18-5

The Danger Zone
Avoid being a World War Two Pilot!
Written by Ian Graham
Illustrated by David Antram
Ian Graham
HB ISBN: 978-1-906714-09-3
PB ISBN: 978-1-906714-10-9

The Danger Zone
Avoid being a Mammoth Hunter!
Written by John Malam
Illustrated by David Antram
John Malam
HB ISBN: 978-1-904642-09-1
PB ISBN: 978-1-904642-10-7

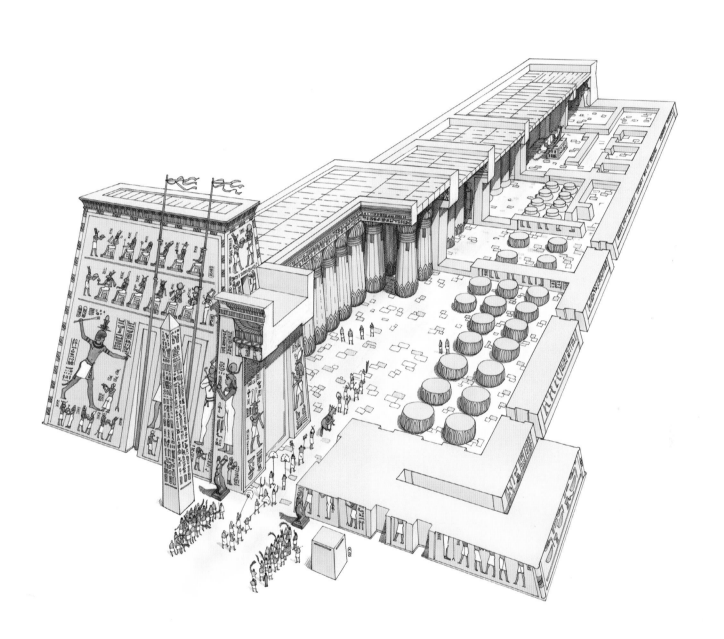

Author:

Jacqueline Morley studied English at Oxford University. She has taught English and History, and now works as a freelance writer. She has written historical fiction and non-fiction for children.

Illustrators:

John James was born in London in 1959. He studied at Eastbourne College of Art and has specialised in historical reconstruction since leaving art school in 1982.

Mark Bergin was born in Hastings, England, in 1961. He studied at Eastbourne College of Art and has specialised in historical reconstructions since leaving art school in 1983.

Series creator:

David Salariya is an illustrator, designer and author. He is the founder of the Salariya Book Company, which specialises in the creation and publication of books for young people, from babies to teenagers, under its imprints Book House, Scribblers and Scribo.

Consultant:

Rosalie David is an Egyptologist at Manchester Museum, and Director of the Manchester Egyptian Mummy Research Project and the Kahun project.

Editor: **Shirley Willis**

Published by
Book House, an imprint of
The Salariya Book Company Ltd
25 Marlborough Place, Brighton BN1 1UB

SALARIYA

Visit our website at **www.book-house.co.uk**
or go to **www.salariya.com**
for **free** electronic versions of:
You Wouldn't Want to be an Egyptian Mummy!
You Wouldn't Want to be a Roman Gladiator!
You Wouldn't Want to be a Polar Explorer!
You Wouldn't Want to sail on a 19th-Century Whaling Ship!

ISBN 978-1-906714-59-8

A CIP catalogue record for this book is available from the British Library.

Printed and bound in China.

CONTENTS

PAPER FROM SUSTAINABLE FORESTS

An Egyptian Pyramid

Written by
Jacqueline Morley

Series created by
David Salariya

Illustrated by
John James
and
Mark Bergin

BOOK HOUSE

INTRODUCTION

THE GREAT PYRAMID OF GIZA, still towering over the desert just as it did when King Khufu (sometimes known as Cheops) built it four and a half thousand years ago, is probably the most famous monument in the world. But did you know that the remains of more than eighty pyramids have been found along the Nile, and that the ancient Egyptians went on building them for a thousand years?

Ancient Egypt's recorded history spans more than three thousand years, from about 3100 BC till 30 BC when Egypt became a part of the Roman Empire. Egyptologists divide this long stretch of time into several periods, calling the three most important ones the Old, Middle and New Kingdoms. The great age of pyramid building was during the Old Kingdom (2686 to 2181 BC) when the Great Pyramid was built, but many later pyramids survive, mostly as heaps of rubble crumbled into the sand.

The pyramid in this book is not based on a particular example but is representative of them all. Evidence from the Middle Kingdom (1991 to 1786 BC) has been used to reconstruct the lives of the pyramid workers, whose way of life, like those of all ordinary people in ancient Egypt, changed little with time. This book answers many of the questions that you may have asked about pyramids – such as, are they hollow? how did people get in? and, above all, why were they built? and how?

THE MEANING OF THE PYRAMID

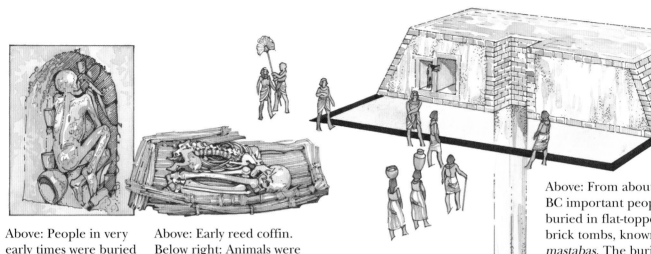

Above: People in very early times were buried in the sand with their possessions for use in the afterlife.

Above: Early reed coffin. Below right: Animals were mummified in later times. 1. Two falcons. 2. An ibis. 3. A calf. 4. A cat.

Above: From about 3100 BC important people were buried in flat-topped, mud-brick tombs, known as *mastabas*. The burial chamber was at the bottom of a deep shaft. Food for the dead person's spirit was placed in a room at ground level. From the next room a statue of the dead person watched through an opening in the wall.

THE ANCIENT EGYPTIANS believed the pharaoh, their king, was the son of the sun god. While he reigned on earth he was Horus, son of the great sun god, Re. When he died he crossed from the land of the living into the Land of the Dead, where he was united with the god Re himself. His successor as pharaoh became the new Horus in this world.

When the sun disappeared in the west the Egyptians thought the sun god was travelling through the night. They knew he would be reborn next morning. They believed when the pharaoh died he would travel into the west with the sun. The Land of the Dead therefore lay in the west, and so the Egyptians buried people on the west side of the River Nile. They built their towns on the east side.

With a god-king who lived for ever, Egypt would enjoy every blessing the gods could give. But to ensure this the pharaoh's body had to be preserved, or his spirit would die. The pyramids were huge, man-made mountains designed to protect the pharaoh's body for ever. Deep inside lay the burial chamber of the king. Although his subjects did not hope to share his godlike immortality, they hoped for some existence beyond the grave. The pyramid was a symbol of such hope. It promised everlasting prosperity by ensuring the pharaoh's union with the gods.

5 **6**

7

5. As time went on, mastabas were made with their upper parts built up in layers, making a sort of pyramid with stepped sides. In about 2646 BC the first step pyramid made of stone was built.

6. At the beginning of the Fourth Dynasty the first true pyramids were built. The Bent Pyramid at Dashur (2589 BC) is so called because the angle of its sides changes halfway up.

7. A cutaway view of a New Kingdom tomb. By 1567 BC pyramids were no longer being built. Instead, royal tombs were cut deep into a rocky hillside. A long passageway led to the burial chamber.

The shape of a pyramid represented the rays of the sun falling on the earth. After his death the pharaoh was thought to mount to heaven on the sun's rays.

LAYING THE FOUNDATIONS

EACH PHARAOH started building his pyramid long before he grew old or expected to die, for it would take many years to finish. He ordered his architect to make designs, and sent officials to the hillside west of the Nile to find a suitable site. It had to be on rocky ground to support the enormous weight of the pyramid, yet not too far from the river, because much of the stone would have to come from the quarries by boat.

When the place had been chosen and the rock cleared of sand, the base of the pyramid was marked out. The sides had to face exactly north, south, east and west, so before work could begin an astronomer priest observed the stars to decide in which direction true north lay. Then the square was marked out with stakes and a measuring cord of palm fibre. This tended to stretch, so it is all the more surprising that although the sides of the Great Pyramid are about 230 metres long, they differ by less than 200 mm.

In theory the pharaoh himself found the site and positioned the pyramid, because being the son of a god he was all-powerful and all-knowing. In practice his officials did the work and the pharaoh re-enacted it symbolically in a special ceremony, rather as an important person today lays the foundation stone of a new building.

Above: The pharaoh instructs his architect. The most famous Egyptian architect was Imhotep, who built the first pyramid for the pharaoh Zoser, in about 2646 BC. Imhotep's fame was legendary. He was thought to have been a magician.

Imhotep is said to have invented the art of building in cut stone. This may be true, for there is no evidence of stone being used in a major way in any earlier building.

Right: The pharaoh arrives to perform the ceremonies that will ensure the goodwill of the gods during the building of his pyramid. He will go through the motions of marking out the site, helped by a priest dressed as Thoth, the scribe-god.

Left: Levelling the site. The channels shown opposite were filled with water. Any rock standing above the waterline was cut away, and the channels were then filled in again with rubble.

Above and left: Finding true north. A circular wall was built to make an artificial horizon. From its centre a priest guided his assistant to mark on the wall the position of a star's appearance.

1: Through a notched staff the priest observed the exact point of the star's rising.
2. Some hours later he observed the point of its setting.
3. Midway between these two points lay the north.

Below: When the position of the pyramid had been marked, a criss-cross of channels was cut across the site in order to level the ground (see explanation, below left). Sometimes only the outer area was levelled, and big outcrops of rock were built into the pyramid to save effort later on.

W *N* *E*

QUARRYING THE STONE

SEVERAL KINDS OF STONE were used in building the pyramid. Local limestone was used for the blocks that made up its core, but the very best limestone was brought across the river from quarries at Tura and the Mugattam hills to make the pyramid's outer casing. Granite was used for important details. The pharaoh's scribes made lists of the amount of stone needed and the sizes of the blocks. These were sent to the overseers in charge of the quarries, who kept careful records of the number of blocks that had been cut and dispatched.

The best limestone lay beneath the surface and was reached by cutting tunnels in the rock. The quarrymen used tools made of a very hard stone called dolerite, or of copper, for people had not yet discovered how to make iron. Copper is softer than iron but the ancient Egyptians may have had special techniques for hardening it.

The quarrymen worked in gangs. They painted the name of their gang on the stones they had cut before these were taken from the quarry, so that the gang's work could be checked. Such names as Boat Gang, Sceptre Gang, Vigorous Gang and Enduring Gang have been found on the stones of the pyramids.

Quarrying limestone.
Stone was cut from near the roof of the quarry first, and then work continued downwards so that quarrymen could crawl across the top of the block and chip it away from the back, while others cut it away from the front. Wooden wedges were driven in to help free the block completely. The wedges were soaked with water which made the wood expand and split the stone away.

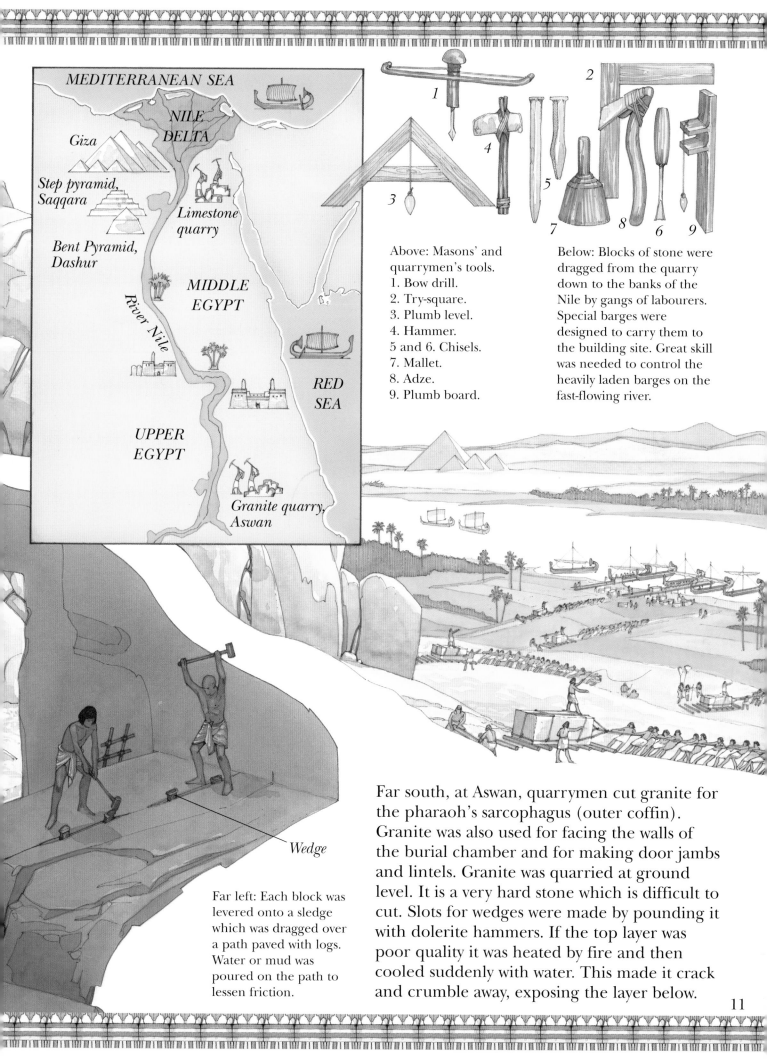

MEDITERRANEAN SEA

NILE DELTA

Giza

Step pyramid, Saqqara

Bent Pyramid, Dashur

Limestone quarry

River Nile

MIDDLE EGYPT

UPPER EGYPT

RED SEA

Granite quarry, Aswan

Above: Masons' and quarrymen's tools.
1. Bow drill.
2. Try-square.
3. Plumb level.
4. Hammer.
5 and 6. Chisels.
7. Mallet.
8. Adze.
9. Plumb board.

Below: Blocks of stone were dragged from the quarry down to the banks of the Nile by gangs of labourers. Special barges were designed to carry them to the building site. Great skill was needed to control the heavily laden barges on the fast-flowing river.

Wedge

Far left: Each block was levered onto a sledge which was dragged over a path paved with logs. Water or mud was poured on the path to lessen friction.

Far south, at Aswan, quarrymen cut granite for the pharaoh's sarcophagus (outer coffin). Granite was also used for facing the walls of the burial chamber and for making door jambs and lintels. Granite was quarried at ground level. It is a very hard stone which is difficult to cut. Slots for wedges were made by pounding it with dolerite hammers. If the top layer was poor quality it was heated by fire and then cooled suddenly with water. This made it crack and crumble away, exposing the layer below.

11

THE PYRAMID RISES

WHEN THE SITE WAS LEVEL, work began on the pyramid itself. If the burial chamber was at ground level, or below ground, as some were, it had to be made first. The sarcophagus was put in place while the chamber was being built, because it was too big to be brought through the entrance passage afterwards. The pyramid was then built up in horizontal layers of stone.

The Egyptians did not use hoisting gear or wheeled vehicles. Stones were dragged into place up ramps, which were built against the side of the pyramid as the building rose. Archaeologists are not sure how the ramps were placed. Some think only one huge ramp was built at right angles to the side. Others believe there were four ramps which began at each corner and ran up the sides.

Causeway

While the site was being prepared, other workers had been making a wide, smooth causeway from the river to the building site so that the stones could be brought up easily.

The main pyramid might have smaller pyramids beside it. When the pyramids were finished the causeway was walled and roofed over and a temple, known as the valley temple, was built on the site of the landing stage.

Causeway

Valley temple

The passage from the burial chamber to the entrance was not cut through the finished pyramid. Instead a gap was left for it in each layer of stone. It was roofed with special slabs to bear the great weight above it. Its entrance was usually sited in the north wall, but some way above ground and not in the middle, so that it would remain well hidden. Great efforts were taken to prevent would-be tomb robbers from looting the royal tomb of its many treasures in later years.

The Great Pyramid of Giza under construction, cut away to show its chambers and passageways. Most of the pyramid was of solid stone. Once the first layer of stone was in place the mud-brick ramps were begun. As each successive layer of stone was laid, the ramps were built higher.

When the gangs had dragged the stones to the top, masons set them in their final places. Wooden rockers which have been found on pyramid sites may have been used to slide the stones into place. Various chambers were enclosed by the stone.

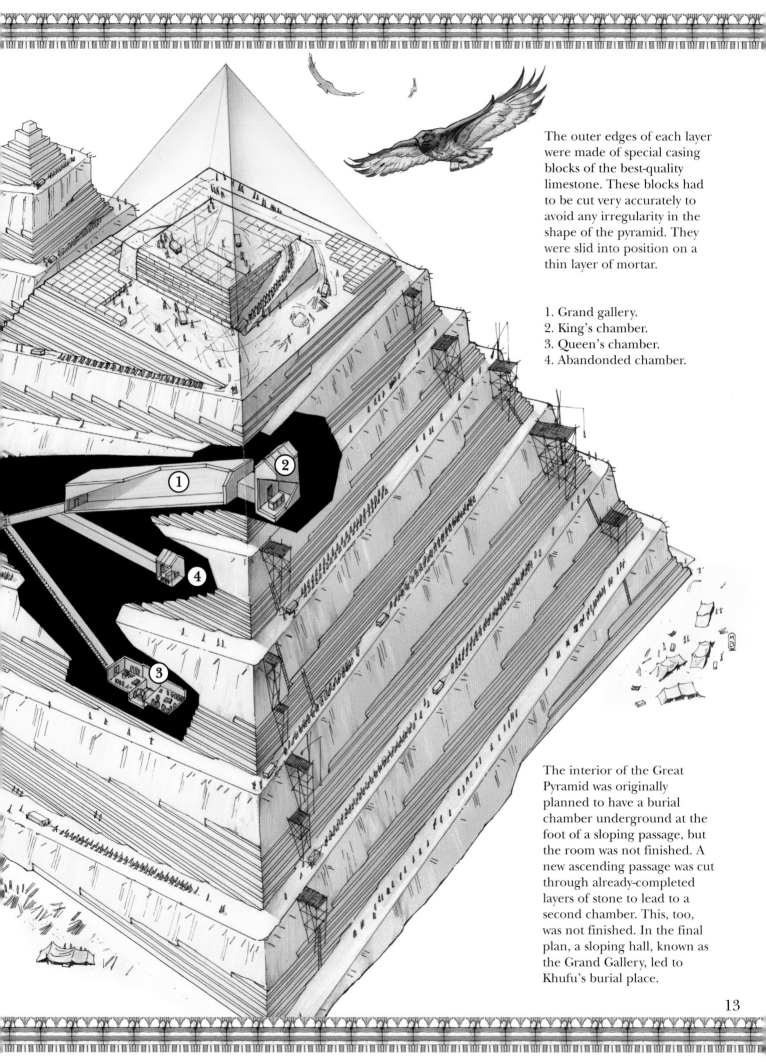

The outer edges of each layer were made of special casing blocks of the best-quality limestone. These blocks had to be cut very accurately to avoid any irregularity in the shape of the pyramid. They were slid into position on a thin layer of mortar.

1. Grand gallery.
2. King's chamber.
3. Queen's chamber.
4. Abandonded chamber.

The interior of the Great Pyramid was originally planned to have a burial chamber underground at the foot of a sloping passage, but the room was not finished. A new ascending passage was cut through already-completed layers of stone to lead to a second chamber. This, too, was not finished. In the final plan, a sloping hall, known as the Grand Gallery, led to Khufu's burial place.

The labourer's year

For much of the year the pyramid workers were farmers. Some worked for themselves, others laboured on estates.

HUGE NUMBERS OF WORKERS were needed to build a pyramid. Highly trained craftsmen cut the stones and laid them in place, but the tiring work of dragging the blocks from the quarry, transporting them to the site, and hauling them from the river and up the ramp was done by gangs of forced labourers. Some of the labourers were convicts or prisoners of war, but most were ordinary peasant farmers. Every year the pharaoh's officials went around the countryside summoning a certain number of men from each village to join the workforce. This was not as wasteful of the farmers' time as you might think, because for several months of the year the River Nile covered the land with floodwater and no farmwork could be done.

The ancient Egyptians divided the year into three seasons: flood, growing time and harvest. Without the rich layer of mud left behind by the Nile's floodwater nothing could be grown, for there was hardly any rain. Not surprisingly, people thought that the flood was sent by the gods, and that if the gods were not pleased the flood would be small or might not come at all. Only a pharaoh could satisfy the gods and ensure a good flood, because he was the son of a god. This was his most important task, for without the flood the land would become a desert and everyone would starve. Because they believed this, people were glad to work for their pharaoh.

1. As soon as the floods went down, the farmers sowed their grain, before the sun baked the earth too hard.

Bullocks pulled wooden ploughs through the soft Nile mud. Animals trod in the seed.

5. Taxmen estimated the farmer's likely crop and told him how much of it he must give to the pharaoh.

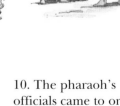

9. When the flood came the houses stood out like islands. People had to travel about in boats.

10. The pharaoh's officials came to order the men of each family to join the pyramid workforce.

2. The peasants had to mend the irrigation canals each year, as part of the tax they paid to the pharaoh.

3. The fields had to be weeded and watered. Men threw stones to scare the birds from the crops.

4. Cows were kept to give milk, but only the owners of large estates could afford to keep herds for meat.

Pigs, sheep, ducks and geese were eaten. Birds were fattened by having food pushed down their throats.

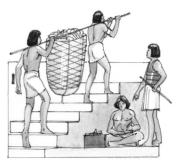

6. At harvest time the corn was cut just below the ear. The sickles were wooden and had flint blades.

7. The corn was beaten with flails on the threshing floor, to separate the grain from the chaff.

Winnowing was done by women. They tossed the grain up in the air and the breeze blew the chaff away.

8. After weighing, the grain was stored in granaries. Tax officials wrote down the quantities.

11. Young boys and old men were left at home. The boys helped the family to earn a living by fishing.

They made boats by lashing papyrus reeds together. They netted the fish or speared them with harpoons.

12. While they waited for the menfolk to return, the women spun and made mats, sandals and baskets.

The older men made tools and repaired broken ones so that everything would be ready for the next season.

A CRAFTSMAN'S DAY

1. The workmen assemble early in the morning. Each gang reports to its own foreman. The scribe checks his list of names to see that everyone is present. One man has sent his wife along to say that he is too ill to come. The scribe writes down the excuse.

I N ADDITION to the peasants who were used to move stones, there were trained craftsmen to do the more skilful work on the pyramid: stonemasons, surveyors and carpenters, metal workers to make and sharpen tools, and stone carvers and painters to decorate the walls of the temples belonging to the pyramid. These men worked all year long at the site. They were housed in barracks close to the pyramid or in towns which had been built especially for them, not far away. The site of a Middle Kingdom pyramid workers' town has been discovered at Kahun in the Fayoum oasis (see pages 18–19).

5. Lunchbreak. The men chat. There is a rumour that the grain to pay their wages has not come.

6. Masons check to see whether a block of stone has been cut accurately. When the roughly hewn blocks come from the quarry they have to be cut to size. This is skilled work.

7. An accident on the ramp. A huge granite slab breaks away and the foreman is hurled to the ground.

Accidents like this were not uncommon. Many families had lost a father or son in a fatal accident at the site.

8. A scribe admits that no grain has come and the men cannot be paid. They call a strike for the next day.

Above: Daily rations of bread, beer and onions.

2. The gang goes to the warehouse where official stores are kept. Each man is issued with tools and his food for the day.

3. The director of building operations discusses the day's work with a foreman. The foreman will then tell his men what to do.

4. A foreman shouts at a gang of peasants. He is angry because the masons at the top of the ramp are waiting for more stone.

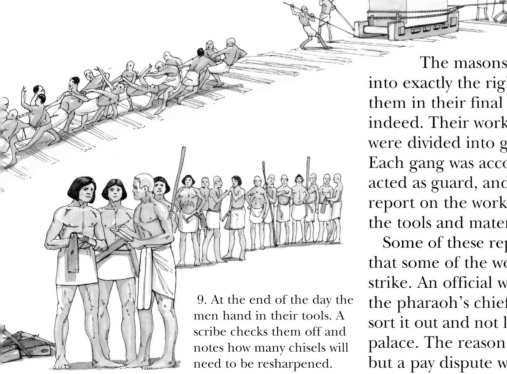

9. At the end of the day the men hand in their tools. A scribe checks them off and notes how many chisels will need to be resharpened.

The masons who cut the rough blocks into exactly the right size and shape, and laid them in their final positions, were very skilled indeed. Their work was strictly controlled. They were divided into gangs, each with a foreman. Each gang was accompanied by a soldier who acted as guard, and a scribe who wrote a daily report on the work carried out by the gang and the tools and materials they had used.

Some of these reports have survived. We know that some of the workers at Kahun went on strike. An official wrote about it to the vizier, the pharaoh's chief minister, and was told to sort it out and not let the protestors come to the palace. The reason for the strike is not known, but a pay dispute was probably the cause of it.

A PLANNED TOWN

IN ABOUT 1895 BC, Sesostris II founded a town on the edge of the desert, at a place now called Kahun, to house the workers who would build his pyramid. Many pharaohs must have done the same. The town was surrounded by a brick wall with a closely guarded gate. Tight security was needed because the pharaohs wanted as few people as possible to know the way into the pyramid to reach their tombs. The craftsmen who knew these secrets were kept away from the people of other towns.

The town was laid out in regular rows of houses which opened onto the street. A drain ran down the middle of each street to prevent it from getting muddy. A palace, which was used by Sesostris II when he inspected his pyramid, stood on a high platform overlooking the rest of the town. Senior officials lived nearby, in grand houses with a large number of rooms. There were offices and reception rooms, a colonnaded courtyard for entertaining guests, a set of private rooms for the owner and another for the women of his family. The best rooms were large and cool, with ceilings supported by columns.

The workmen's houses were in a separate part of the town. Some had only four rooms, but the flat roofs provided additional space for living, working and sleeping. Cooking was done over a fire made in a shallow dip in the floor of the kitchen.

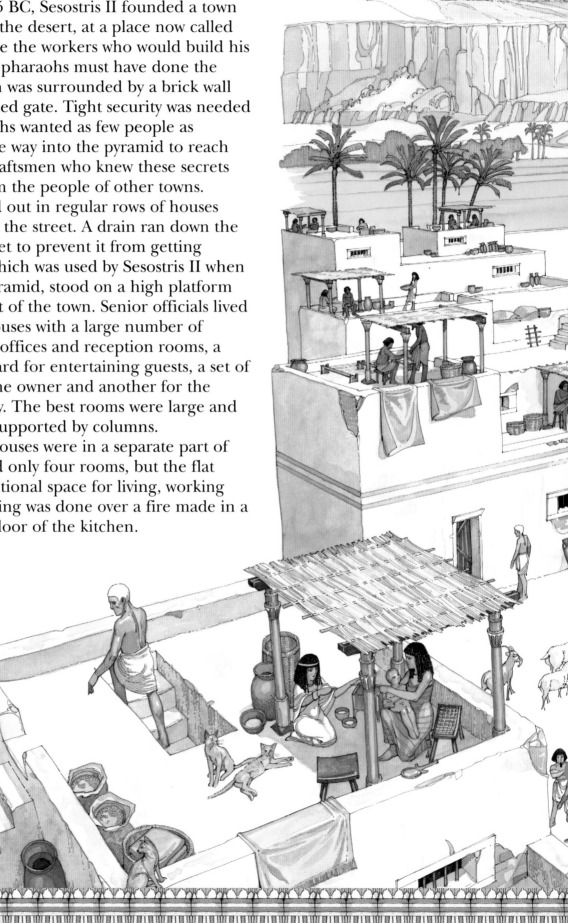

The town of Kahun was excavated by the British archaeologist William Flinders Petrie. He worked on the site for two seasons, 1888–1889 and 1889–1890. At the time when Sesostris founded the town it was named Hetep-Sesostris, meaning 'Sesostris is satisfied'. Kahun is a later, Arabic name. The town stood close to the valley temple of Sesostris.

The town was probably laid out by the architect who designed Sesostris' pyramid. Petrie was very excited by the thought of what he might find there. This was the first time that a complete Egyptian town had been uncovered. Until then, most of what people knew about ancient Egypt had been based on evidence from tombs and temples.

Petrie made his workmen inspect every inch of the soil that they dug, and paid them extra money for every object that they discovered. He paid highly for pieces of papyrus and bronze tools. Petrie uncovered the remains of over two thousand rooms, in an area which formed about three-quarters of the town. The remainder was too worn away to be excavated.

Petrie found tools and furniture such as small offering tables, stone and wooden seats, and coffers. He even found children's toys: balls, spinning tops and board games, and little animals that they had made for themselves out of clay. Afterwards the rooms were covered over with earth in order to protect them. Today the site is once more buried in the sand.

19

THE PEOPLE OF THE TOWN

The governor of the town, with his wife and son, in the courtyard of their fine house.

Rich Egyptians wore clothes of fine pleated linen. Children wore few clothes.

Priests of Sesostris' mortuary temple, near his pyramid, where they held ceremonies in his honour.

Priests also worshipped at Sesostris' valley temple which stood where the Nile's floodwater met the desert.

THE TOWN WAS RULED by the governor, who lived in a fine house. He received his orders from the vizier and was responsible for all supplies that came into the town. He was also in charge of law and order but, like the pharaoh, he had many important officials to help him. They lived in the town too.

Priests were important in the community. They could marry, and their sons often became priests. They performed daily rituals in the temple and ran the town's schools.

The town had doctors whose writings have survived. The Egyptians understood quite a lot about how the body works, because they opened bodies to clean them out before mummification (see pages 38–39).

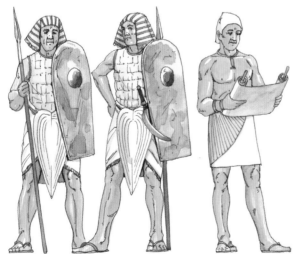

Many soldiers were stationed in the town. The pharaoh kept his workers under strict control.

The warehouse foreman was a familiar figure. He gave out the workers' tools and rations each day.

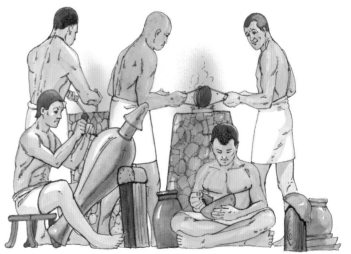

Goldsmiths at work. One chases an inscription onto a vase. Others are working over a small furnace.

A scribe records the gold issued. The finished article will be weighed, to prevent the theft of gold.

Head of the Legal Office, Captain of the Guard, Controller of Stores, Temple Superintendent.

Temple records show that the Superintendent earned eight jugs of beer and sixteen loaves daily.

Amongst the buildings of the temple is the school with about twenty small boys in each classroom.

The temples also employed dancers and singers who performed at the festivals in honour of the gods.

Most of the town's workers were employed on the pyramid in one way or another. There were craftsmen of many kinds, soldiers who policed the town and worksite, keepers of the building supplies and a great number of scribes to keep records. Other townsfolk made essential things like cloth, pottery and furniture which they sold in the town.

All depended on the local farmers who provided food. They also supplied the priests with food for the offerings made daily in the temple. Some people, but not many, may have been foreigners. The people of Kahun must have been proud of their town. Records show that many of them called their sons Sesostris, after the town's founder.

Townspeople worked hard, except on holidays. Children helped by minding the animals.

A farmer and a cloth merchant at the market. Animals provided meat, milk and clothing.

Wool was worn by ordinary people. Priests never wore it because it was thought to be ritually unclean.

Foreign pottery found at Kahun suggests that some people had come from nearby countries to find work.

Life in the Town

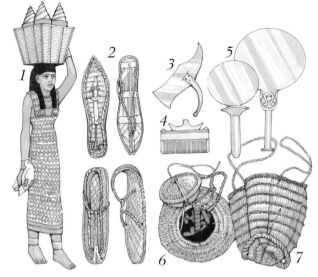

1. Figure of a woman bringing goods to market.
2. Sandals.
3. A razor.
4. A comb.
5. Copper mirrors, one with the head of the goddess Hathor on the handle.
6. A basket.
7. A bag made of twine.

THE PEOPLE OF KAHUN probably did not mind their isolation, for the town was a lively world in itself. The centre of town life was the market where people brought goods to exchange. The ancient Egyptians did not use money. Wages were paid in food and clothing.

The market stalls were set out along the streets. Farmers came with donkeys laden with fruit, vegetables and grain. Some brought geese and game birds, but not chickens; the Egyptians did not have these until about 1550 BC, when they were introduced from Syria. Others brought fish they had caught or goods they had made at home: sandals, cloth and things to eat and drink, mostly bread, cakes, wine and beer. There was a lot of arguing about the value of the goods being exchanged, and an official market attendant kept order and looked out for shoplifters.

Specialist craftsmen had stalls, too. Beads, jewellery and cosmetics were sold. A painted wooden doll with movable arms and legs was found at Kahun, and a large stock of doll's hair was discovered in what must have been the doll maker's shop.

Even when the pyramid was finished the town continued to be busy. Priests and their attendants were always needed to perform the rituals of the mortuary temple, and many craftsmen were employed in maintaining Sesostris' monuments.

Above: People exchanging goods. The price of an object in the market was made up of the goods the seller would take in exchange.

Below: The market, where most trade was done. There were no shops like those of today, though craftsmen sold goods at their doors.

Hunting was a favourite pastime. The fertile area around the nearby Fayoum oasis was a haven for wildlife. Wealthy people also liked to hunt gazelles, leopards, ibex and wild ox in the desert. Hounds drove the game into nets, where they were shot with bows and arrows.

Above: Netting birds in the marshy thickets. At flood time the lakes made by the Nile's waters were full of wild fowl.

Right: A fishing party on the Nile. Poorer people also went hunting to obtain some additional food.

Below: Treading grapes for wine. Most farmers grew a few vines. The wine was stored in narrow-necked jars, sealed with mud.

Left and above: Beer making. Bread was crumbled into a liquid sweetened with dates. The lumpy beer was strained after fermenting.

THE WORKSHOPS

THE TOWN OF KAHUN was full of workshops. The craftsmen who worked in them made everything needed in the town as well as at the pyramid. Stoneworkers not only shaped huge blocks of stone, they were also amazingly skilful at hollowing out hard stone to form vases and tiny cosmetic jars.

Brick makers were kept busy, for pyramids were no longer made entirely of stone as they had been in Old Kingdom times. Although Sesostris' pyramid was faced with stone, the inside consisted of thousands of bricks made from Nile mud, pressed into moulds and dried in the sun. Bricks lasted in the dry climate of Egypt without needing to be baked in a kiln.

Metal workers made tools, weapons and jars by hammering copper, or by casting molten copper in clay moulds. Many craftsmen made decorative objects for the tombs. Carpenters and goldsmiths made coffins, amulets and funeral goods as well as furniture and jewellery for the wealthy.

Above: Painters decorating a tomb. In the Middle Kingdom (1991–1786 BC) many tombs were brightly decorated with scenes of daily life and objects that the dead person might need.

The artist was given a sketch of the design to be painted, marked in squares to help him copy the design. He drew a grid on the wall with a piece of string soaked in paint.

Left: A bundle of brushes, used for marking lines, found tied up with a rope. The wooden palette held cakes of paint and has a slot for brushes in use.

Above: Carpenters, from a wall painting.

Left: Carpenters' workshop. One is using an adze and another a bow drill. A man saws through wood which is held steady by lashing it to a plank. He has left his saw in the cut while he adjusts the position of the wood.

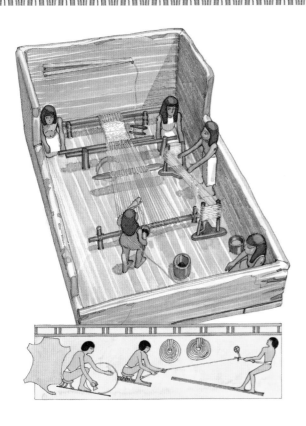

Metal working. Copper was smelted over a bellows-powered furnace, and poured through funnels into moulds.

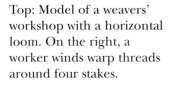

Top: Model of a weavers' workshop with a horizontal loom. On the right, a worker winds warp threads around four stakes.

Above: Making rope from leather. On the left, a leather worker; on the right, two men twisting the strands of rope together.

Above: Axe blades cast in moulds were sharpened to produce cutting edges. The blades were lashed to the wooden handles by thongs.

Below: Goldsmiths pour molten gold into a mould. In the foreground one is shaping a dish from a sheet of metal.

Many people helped to make cloth, especially linen, for which Egypt was famous. Spinning was done by women at home whenever they had a spare moment. Weaving was more professional work, for looms took up a lot of room and usually belonged to full-time weavers, generally women. The preparation of the flax fibres and the finishing of the cloth were done by specialist craftsmen. Fine linen was valuable and was often given as wages.

Above: A model of potters at work. One is preparing clay while another is turning the wheel with one hand and shaping the pot with the other.

Left: Making stone vases. The drill was weighted with stones, which acted as a flywheel to give a regular movement.

THE FESTIVAL OF BES

THE ANCIENT EGYPTIANS liked to enjoy themselves. We know from their drawings and inscriptions that they loved singing, dancing, eating and drinking. The festivals of the gods were holidays when everyone had a good time.

The ancient Egyptians worshipped many different gods. Some important and powerful gods were known throughout Egypt, while others were honoured in particular places. The most important gods were worshipped in great temples looked after by rich and powerful priests. Only the pharaoh and the priests were allowed to take part in the ceremonies in the temples; ordinary people could only bring offerings into the entrance courts.

Egyptians felt that these great gods were too remote to be interested in the everyday troubles of ordinary people. But there were a number of other, more homely gods, who were kind and protected ordinary people, although they did not have grand temples. Amongst these gods were Bes the dwarf, and Tauert who cared for women in childbirth.

Bes was associated with feasting and fun. People painted his likeness inside their houses and wore amulets in his image to ward off dangers – snakes, scorpions and evil spirits. A dancer's mask with the face of Bes, and a pair of ivory dancing clappers have been found in a house at Kahun, so we know that celebrations in his honour were held there.

Dancers depicted in a carving on the side of a chair. They represent Bes and Tauert. Bes had the mane, ears and tail of a lion. Tauert was thought of as a pregnant hippopotamus.

The Egyptians worshipped many gods. In early times each region had possessed its own gods and legends. In about 3100 BC a legendary pharaoh is said to have joined all the regions into one kingdom. After this, stories about the gods were shared and beliefs were intermixed. Important gods had festival days when priests would carry the god's image through the streets and there was a great celebration. The statue was carried in a shrine because it was too sacred for ordinary people to look at. The friendly household gods, like Bes, did not have great festivals organised by the priests. The people honoured them in unofficial ways.

Right: No work is being done on the pyramid today, for the townspeople are holding a celebration in honour of Bes. Dancers lead the procession, wearing masks representing Bes, Tauert and their attendants. They beat tambourines and strike clappers together. The townspeople follow, singing, or join in from the rooftops. Children skip beside the dancers.

PHARAOH AND HIS COURT

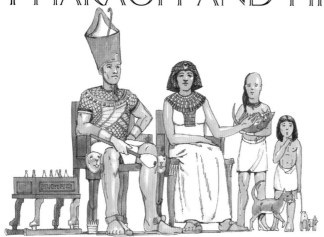

The pharaoh and his family. He is wearing the red and white double crown, symbol of the union of Upper and Lower Egypt.

If the pharaoh died while his eldest son was still a child, the queen became regent and ruled on his behalf.

The court had many ceremonies. This rich man has the title of Royal Fan Bearer, but the post does not involve any real work.

The pharaoh's chief officials: the Overseer of the Treasury, the Master of Building Works and the Head of the Law Courts.

THE WORD *PHARAOH* means 'great house'. Egyptians believed there was no limit to a pharaoh's greatness. As god-king he was all-powerful. The land and everything in it belonged to him. His people had to obey his commands in all things. In return he obtained the blessing of the gods for Egypt so that the country prospered.

The pharaoh decided all important matters. He was head of the government and the legal system, chief priest of all the temples and head of the army. He controlled the mines and the quarries and all building projects. He regulated trade. He stored all the surplus grain in his granaries and controlled the irrigation system that watered the fields.

The Chief Secretary wrote letters dictated by the pharaoh. His office stored the royal correspondence.

Servants of the royal household: the Head Baker, the Chief Cook, and the Butler carrying wine.

The pharaoh's many personal servants dressed him and waited on him, and looked after his possessions.

Porters carried his litter. Standard bearers and fan bearers attended him wherever he went.

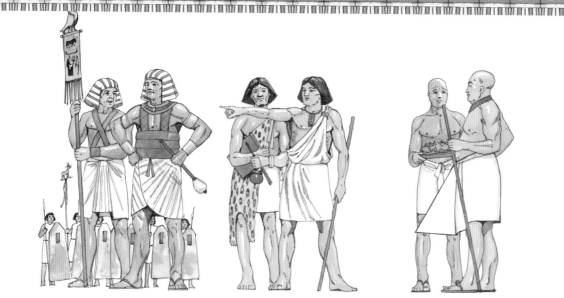

The Commander of the Army. An army was organised only when it was needed, until the New Kingdom when a permanent army was formed.

The Chief of Irrigation kept the floodwater canals in permanent repair. The Overseer of Granaries stored the harvest.

The chief priest of the most important god was very influential. The pharaoh had to stop him gaining too much power.

A regional governor. Governors were originally hereditary princes, but these grew too powerful and were replaced by appointed officials.

Of course, no pharaoh could possibly do all this work himself. He had thousands of officials who did it for him. The most important of these was the vizier. The business of government was directed by the vizier, who kept his eye on every department and reported every day to the pharaoh on the affairs of the kingdom.

Past pharaohs had often given grants of land, and peasants to work on it, to their high officials and to the temples. In theory the land still belonged to the ruling pharaoh, but in practice it made many of his subjects very rich. These rich nobles and important priests held high positions in the government and at the pharaoh's court.

Court musicians play to entertain the pharaoh. One girl plays the flute and another the harp.

A young girl sings and accompanies herself on the lute. A lyre player kneels beside her.

Dancers and acrobats were also called upon to provide entertainment for guests at feasts.

Some of the dances were very energetic. Skilled acrobats leapt and turned somersaults.

THE PHARAOH'S DAY

ON WAKING, the pharaoh reads the letters brought in by his secretary and dictates his replies. Then he is bathed by his servants and dressed in his state clothes and official regalia. Next he receives his vizier, who reports to him on all the important business of the kingdom. Afterwards he hears petitions from his subjects and gives judgement on legal matters. He may also have a visit from a foreign ambassador or a trade delegation from another country.

The pharaoh reads through a letter that he has just dictated. It will be cut from the papyrus, folded, tied and sealed.

The pharaoh is dressed. His toilet has been performed by his barber and his manicurist. He wears a ceremonial crown.

When his official business is over the pharaoh likes to go hunting in the desert for gazelles and antelope; but today he has to attend an important ceremony. His pyramid, after many years, has been built almost to the top. The granite capstone which forms its point is ready to be placed in position. As in all great undertakings, the pharaoh's power is essential for success in placing the stone.

After making offerings to the gods to ensure their co-operation, the pharaoh will be carried in procession to the pyramid, where the capstone, which has been dragged up the ramp in readiness, is already resting in position on wooden blocks. When the signal is given, workmen will pull the blocks away and the stone will drop into place. A projection on its base will fit into a hole in the top of the pyramid. Afterwards there will be prayers of thanksgiving and a celebration at the palace.

Above: The pharaoh receives ambassadors from a nearby ruler who would like to make a trading treaty with Egypt. They bring gifts.

Below: The capstone ceremony. Peasants have already done the hard work of dragging the massive stone up to the top.

Before the ceremony the pharaoh makes offerings of food and drink before the shrine of the god.

Most pyramid capstones are now missing. An inscription has been found that suggests that some may have been gilded.

The Cairo museum possesses a magnificent Middle Kingdom capstone of about 1700 BC. Each side has an inscription suitable for the direction it faced. The eastern one addresses the rising sun.

Above: After the ceremony the pharaoh and his court enjoy a celebratory banquet. The banqueting hall is a lofty pillared room open along one side and overlooking a cool courtyard.

The guests are sitting on low seats or on the floor. The ancient Egyptians did not eat their meals around large tables. Servants will bring dishes of meat, cakes and fruit and set them on little tables by the guests.

FINISHING TOUCHES

As the pharaoh's mortuary temple was built, mounds of earth were piled against it so that the stones for the next stage of building could be hauled up. When building work was finished, the earth enabled the craftsmen who decorated the temple to reach its topmost parts. They worked from the top downwards, while the earth was being cleared away.

Pillars and ceilings were painted. The Egyptians preferred to decorate the walls with carvings in low relief. Pictures were painted on them if the stone was too soft to carve satisfactorily. The design was first drawn on the wall. The sculptor cut along the lines and rounded the edges of the figures to make them lifelike. Carvings were usually painted.

The mortuary temple had an entrance hall, an open court, storerooms and a sanctuary. The Fifth Dynasty mortuary temple of King Sahure (about 2474 BC) had a courtyard paved with polished basalt. The cloister around the court had a star-spangled ceiling and walls carved with magnificent reliefs showing the king triumphing over his enemies.

Top right, opposite page: Shallow sockets dug into the rock at the corners of the Great Pyramid were designed to hold the four cornerstones. The sockets were cut through the bottom layer of stones. This may have been done to withstand the thrust caused by any eventual sliding of the pyramid, although the sockets seem too shallow for this purpose.

Socket   *Lowest cornerstone*   *Socket for next layer*

WHEN THE CAPSTONE was in place, work began on trimming and polishing the casing stones of the pyramid. The area just below the capstone was dressed first and work continued downwards. Workmen began by dismantling the top of the supply ramp, exposing the casing stones for 6 metres or so. Scaffolding was then put up over the exposed area so that as many men as possible could work on the stone. Stonemasons chiselled away the steps of the casing and then ground and polished the surface smooth, using pieces of stone and abrasive powder. As each layer was finished, more of the supply ramp was dismantled and

the scaffolding was re-erected lower down. This work was repeated until the ramp had been removed entirely and the whole pyramid was smooth and gleaming white.

To the east of the pyramid, workers were finishing the pharaoh's mortuary temple. This was the home of his *ka.* The ancient Egyptians believed that each person possessed various spiritual forces which survived death. One of these was the ka, which was a sort of spiritual double which looked like its owner. It was essential for the dead person's wellbeing that his ka should be given offerings of food every day. In the mortuary temple a statue of the ka helped the priests to lure it back from the underworld so that it could be fed.

PRIESTS AND SCRIBES

EVERY TOWN and settlement in Egypt had a temple dedicated to its local god or family of gods. According to legend the gods had once lived on earth and were now in the Land of the Dead. The temple was the home of the ka of its particular god. Each day the priests took the god's image from its shrine, washed it and dressed it and offered it food.

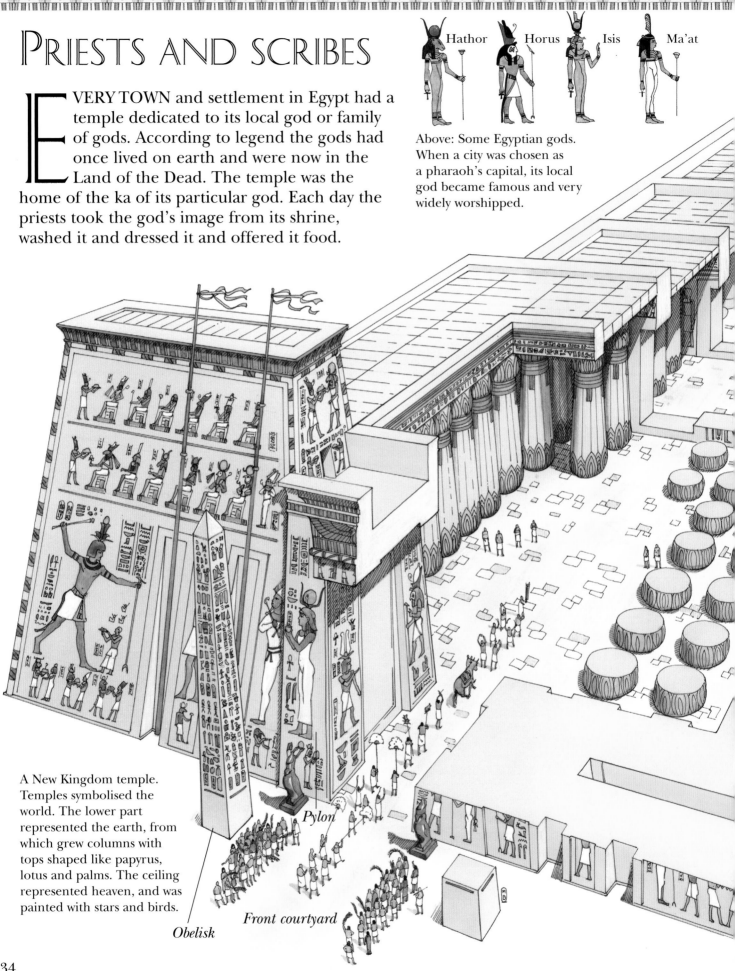

Hathor   Horus   Isis   Ma'at

Above: Some Egyptian gods. When a city was chosen as a pharaoh's capital, its local god became famous and very widely worshipped.

A New Kingdom temple. Temples symbolised the world. The lower part represented the earth, from which grew columns with tops shaped like papyrus, lotus and palms. The ceiling represented heaven, and was painted with stars and birds.

Pylon

Obelisk

Front courtyard

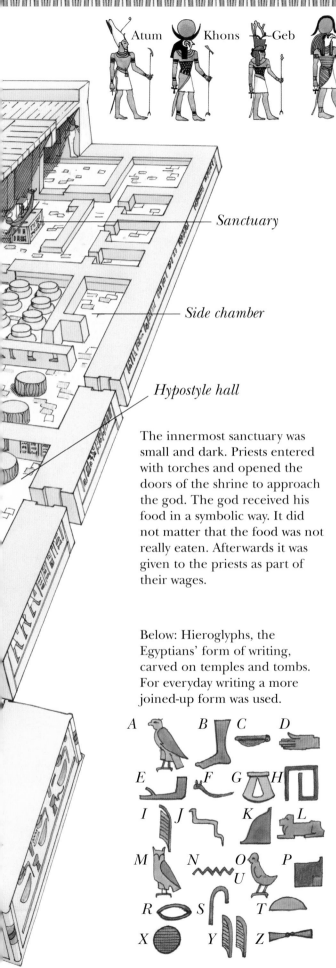

Atum   Khons   Geb   Harakhty   Osiris

Sanctuary

Side chamber

Hypostyle hall

The innermost sanctuary was small and dark. Priests entered with torches and opened the doors of the shrine to approach the god. The god received his food in a symbolic way. It did not matter that the food was not really eaten. Afterwards it was given to the priests as part of their wages.

Below: Hieroglyphs, the Egyptians' form of writing, carved on temples and tombs. For everyday writing a more joined-up form was used.

A   B   C   D

E   F   G   H

I   J   K   L

M   N   O   P
U

R   S   T

X   Y   Z

Papermaking tools

Splitting reeds

Mould

The ancient Egyptians invented paper. They made it from the pith of papyrus reeds which grew in the marshes. Strips were soaked in water and laid in a mould. They were hammered and dried to make sheets and then rolled up.

Below: Gathering bundles of papyrus. The man on the right is peeling the outer covering from the stalk of the reed.

The temples of a great city like Sesostris II's capital at Lisht were more magnificent than those of a little town like Kahun but they were all built to much the same plan. Inside the temple, the sanctuary of the god was approached through a series of courtyards and hypostyle halls (halls with many columns).

The temple stood in a walled enclosure and was surrounded by many buildings, forming a large estate. There were farms to provide food for the god and for his priests and attendants, as well as workshops to supply all their needs. The estate employed many craftsmen and workers and was like a small town. The priests ran schools and trained older boys to become professional record keepers and letter writers, known as scribes. These were essential because not everyone could read and write. Becoming a scribe was the first step in any profession, for officials had to keep detailed records, so that their superiors could report to the vizier on the progress of work.

CROSSING THE RIVER

WHEN A PHARAOH DIED he was taken for the last time across the Nile to the west bank, the Land of the Dead. All Egyptians were buried in the west and had to make this crossing. It was a sacred journey, recalling the voyage of the sun god who crossed the sky daily in a boat.

The pharaoh's body was ferried in a special state boat to the landing stage at the foot of the causeway leading to his pyramid. The quayside, which had once been a busy and untidy place where building stones for the pyramid had been unloaded, had been tidied up long ago and a fine temple now stood there, on a terrace. The pharaoh's names and titles were carved around the doorway and there were many statues of him within. In this temple priests performed ceremonies by which the pharaoh's body was symbolically purified to make it fit to join the gods. His spirit was revived by this cleansing, just as the sun god was reborn each morning by bathing in a sacred lake before beginning his daily journey across the heavens.

Right: A dead pharaoh is taken across the river to his valley temple. In the illustration the large boat which bears his body is based on the one found near Khufu's pyramid. The boat was about 45 metres long and made of cedar wood. Its narrow shape had evolved to navigate the Nile's swift currents, and its tapered stem and sternpost were influenced by earlier boats made from bundles of papyrus.

Above: A funeral procession, from a wall painting in a tomb. Oxen pull a sledge on which the ritual funeral boat is being dragged down to the river. It will then be ferried across on a larger vessel, accompanied by mourners. A priest walks before it.

The washing and mummification of the pharaoh's body were probably carried out in the buildings attached to the temple. On the day of the funeral, the mummy in its coffin was carried along the causeway to the pyramid by a procession of mourners and priests. The causeway was completely enclosed to hide the coffin from view.

Models of funeral boats were often put in tombs in place of real ones. To ancient Egyptians a model or a picture of an object was just as effective, for magic purposes, as the thing itself.

Models were used to provide many of the things which the Egyptians believed a dead person would need in the afterlife. Model houses, model servants and model food have all been found in tombs.

MUMMIFICATION

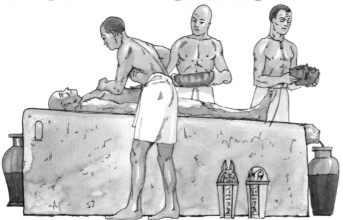

Embalmers at work. The body is placed on the stone embalming table.

The body is opened and cleaned. The brain is removed through the nose.

Above right: The corpse is packed in natron (soda) for 40 days to dry it out.

Below: Amulets (charms) placed within the bandages to give magic protection.

MUMMIES GET THEIR NAME from the Arabic word *mummiya*, meaning 'bitumen'. This is because the resin with which some mummies were filled turned them black over the centuries until they looked like bitumen. Medieval doctors believed that the 'bitumen' would cure illnesses, and for this reason mummies were sent to Europe where they were ground up and swallowed as medicine in the Middle Ages, and even later.

In ancient Egypt mummies served a very different purpose. People believed that after death the soul would perish if it did not have its body to rest in. It was therefore vital to stop the body decaying by making it into what we now call a mummy. Embalmers dried, preserved and wrapped the body before it was returned to the relatives for burial.

In early burials, until about 3000 BC, bodies were preserved naturally in their sand graves – corpses will not rot in very dry conditions. In tombs, bodies did not dry so well, and had to be wrapped in resin-soaked linen and covered with plaster. The earliest pharaohs of the Old Kingdom (2688 to 2181 BC) may have been mummified like this, but we cannot be sure because no mummies have been found in the pyramid burial chambers – they were robbed long ago. Many of the mummies that archaeologists have found date from the New Kingdom or later, when mummification was a much more elaborate process.

Right: Wrapping the mummy took about 15 days. The body had to be bound very tightly to keep its shape. Hundreds of metres of linen were used in up to twenty layers of shrouds and bandages. If, by accident, some part of the body rotted and fell off, or was snatched by a jackal when no-one was looking, the embalmers replaced it with linen wads or wood.

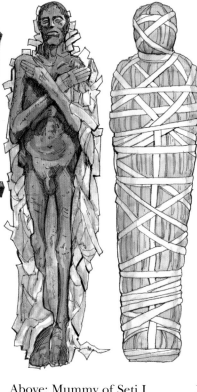

New Kingdom canopic jars and chest. The internal organs, which would have made the mummy rot, were stored in these. The human-headed jar held the liver, the jackal the stomach, the falcon the intestines, and the baboon held the lungs.

Above: Mummy of Seti I (about 1304 BC).
Above right: The mummy's outer shroud, held in place by bandages.

Inner mummy-shaped coffin. This developed in the Middle Kingdom from the mask that covered the face.

Outer coffin made from a hollowed log. It is gilded and decorated with a design of vulture feathers.

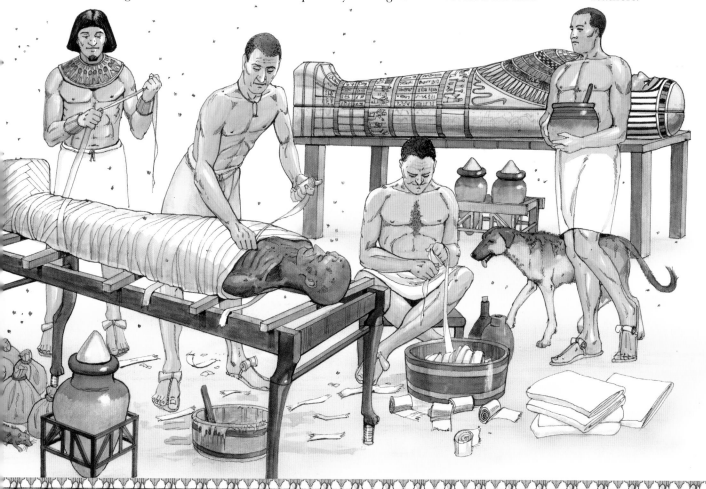

THE CITY OF THE DEAD

A PYRAMID did not stand alone on the hillside. It was surrounded by many other buildings. In addition to the mortuary temple and small side temples there were often one or more smaller pyramids. Archaeologists used to think that these were the pyramids of queens but now they believe they may have held the king's canopic jars – jars containing his organs. Around the pyramid, the low, flat mastaba tombs of the pharaoh's relations and courtiers were laid out in avenues.

The Sphinx, an enormous man-headed lion, lies crouched near the valley temple of Khafre. In Egyptian mythology the lion was a guardian of sacred places. Its head represents a pharaoh, perhaps Khafre or one of his brothers. The statue was carved out of rock left behind by earlier builders when quarrying for stone. Traces of red and yellow show that it was originally painted.

Building the stone pyramids of the Old Kingdom required enormous numbers of men and great skill. The temples and causeway walls were often decorated with figures of the pharaoh and the gods, carved in low relief and painted, and some temples were entirely faced with granite. Some of the blocks in the mortuary temple of Menkaure weigh as much as 220 tonnes each. Granite slabs of over 30 tonnes were brought almost 1,000 kilometres from Aswan.

The pharaohs could not have created these amazing monuments if they had not been able to force their peasants to do dangerous and exhausting work. Yet it would be wrong to suppose that the people thought of their king as a feared and hated tyrant. They believed that by helping their pharaoh to live for ever they helped Egypt to be glorious. From Middle Kingdom times (about 1991 BC) they began to hope for a place in the Land of the Dead – not among the gods like their pharaoh, but happily cultivating the fields.

The pyramids of Giza. In the foreground is the Great Pyramid, built in about 2566 BC by Khufu (Cheops), a pharaoh of the Fourth Dynasty. In the centre is that of his son Khafre (Chephren), and, beyond, that of Menkaure (Mycerinus), who may have been Khafre's brother or son.

Valley temples

Sphinx

In 1954 archaeologists found a sealed boat pit near the Great Pyramid. Inside there was not a complete boat but 1,224 pieces of wood, carefully laid out in 13 layers, together with ropes for rigging, baskets and matting. It took ten years to work out how this, the world's oldest construction kit, fitted together. The puzzle was finally solved, and Khufu's boat is now in a purpose-built museum beside his pyramid.

Right inset: Lowering a boat into its pit. Pits for burying boats have been found near several pyramids. A pharaoh would have needed a boat in the afterlife in order to travel through the sky with the sun. Khufu's boat may have been the state boat used at his funeral.

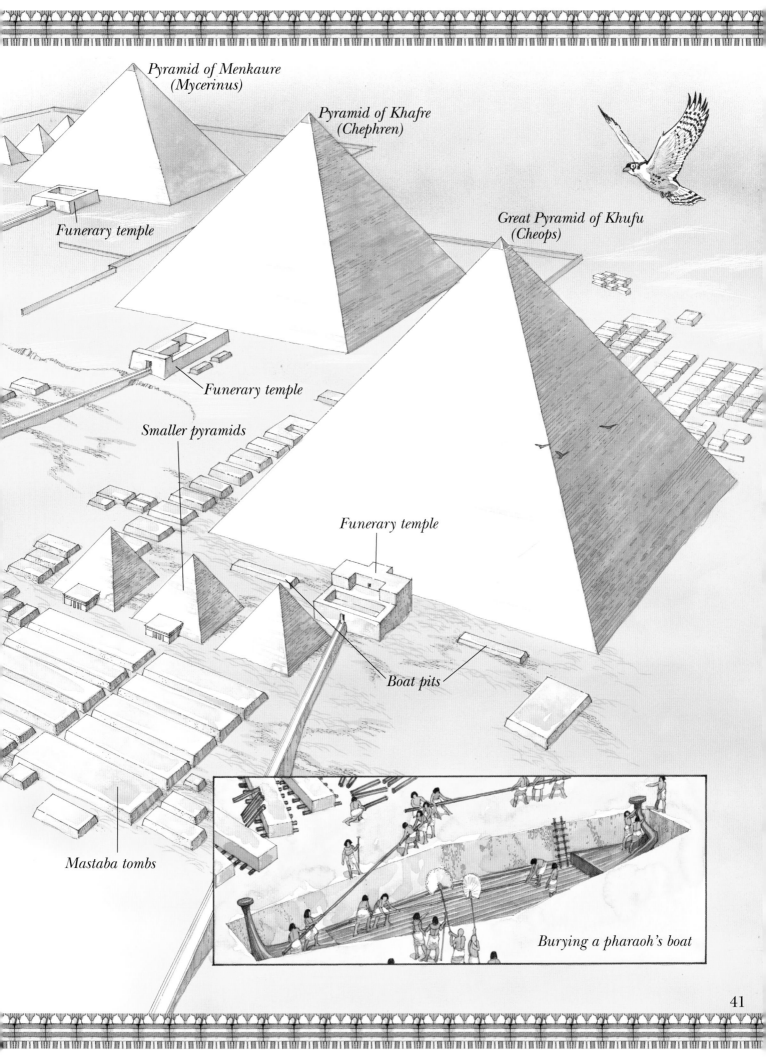

Pyramid of Menkaure
(Mycerinus)

Pyramid of Khafre
(Chephren)

Funerary temple

Great Pyramid of Khufu
(Cheops)

Funerary temple

Smaller pyramids

Funerary temple

Boat pits

Mastaba tombs

Burying a pharaoh's boat

41

Sealing the Tomb

Above: The ceremony of the Opening of the Mouth.

Right: Models of ritual objects used during the ceremony: an adze, an alabaster tray with depressions for the seven sacred oils, and model implements.

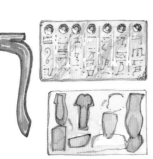

ON THE DAY of the funeral the mummy in its coffin was carried in procession to the mortuary temple. Here the ceremony of the Opening of the Mouth was performed. Priests, one of whom was the son of the dead pharaoh, touched the features and hands of the pharaoh's mummy with ritual implements, and recited prayers. This ceremony gave back to the mummy all its bodily senses so that the pharaoh would be able to eat, speak and move in the afterlife.

Then the mummy in its coffin was placed on a sledge and dragged up a temporary ramp which led up to the entrance of the pyramid. Priests carried the coffin through the narrow passages to the burial chamber and lowered it into the waiting sarcophagus, which was covered with a heavy stone lid. Food and drink were placed in the burial chamber, and the storerooms were filled with magnificent furniture, weapons, clothes and jewellery for the pharaoh to use in the afterlife. Then the mourners withdrew and the entrance to the tomb was sealed.

The utmost precautions were taken to make sure that no-one could enter the pyramid later, to spoil its purity or steal the pharaoh's treasure. The passageway was blocked with stone slabs, and a casing stone was placed over the entrance to match the others. Some pyramids had passages with false doors and dead ends, to foil thieves.

Left: Section of the King's Chamber in the Great Pyramid. The huge stones withstood the weight above.

Above: From Middle Kingdom times Egyptians thought their souls would be weighed in judgement in the afterlife.

The Great Pyramid was sealed by huge granite plugs which had been stored in the Grand Gallery (1). They were released to block the ascending passage (2). The men who released them escaped down a narrow hidden shaft (3) into the lower passage.

Below: How a stone portcullis was dropped into place to seal a chamber.

Even at the time when the pyramids were being built, people began trying to find ways into them. It was well known that they were packed with precious objects and valuable linen.

In spite of all the ways in which the architects tried to foil them, thieves always managed to break in. No doubt at times the craftsmen who built the tombs betrayed their secrets.

Papyrus records tell of the trial of tomb robbers during New Kingdom times. The culprits were temple employees and local townspeople. Senior workmen were fired.

Above: Soldiers policing the royal tombs have caught men who appeared to be trying to force their way in. The vizier has come in person to interrogate them.

TREASURE FOR ETERNITY

Annexe

Antechamber

THE PHARAOH'S EXPENSES in raising a pyramid did not end when the building was finished. The pharaoh also had to make endowments to provide an income for the priests of his mortuary temple who would keep his cult going for eternity. This perhaps explains why later pharaohs, when Egypt was less prosperous, no longer built pyramids, or else made them smaller. Some pyramids were built of rubble and mud brick, with only a facing of limestone. When the facing blocks came off, the insides gradually crumbled away.

Opposite page: Howard Carter and his patron, Lord Carnarvon, together with Lord Carnarvon's daughter and two assistants, at the door of the tomb. They found that it had been entered and resealed in antiquity. The first room was packed with objects which were piled on top of each other in confusion as if the robbers had been caught in the act by the tomb guards.

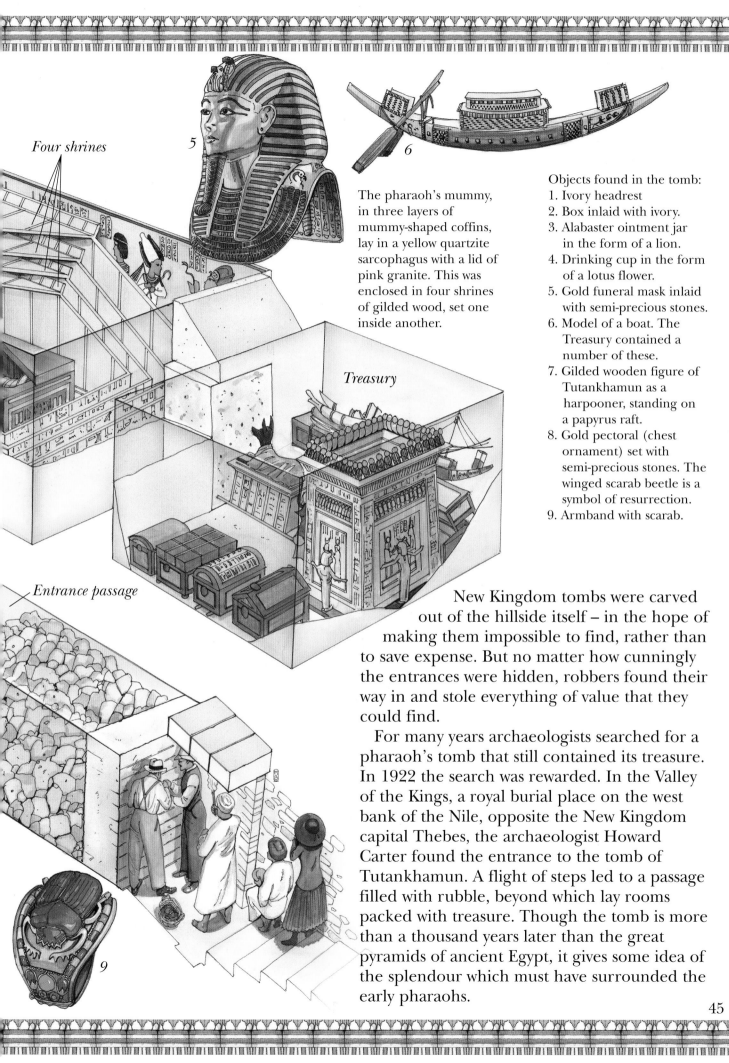

Four shrines

5

6

Entrance passage

Treasury

9

The pharaoh's mummy, in three layers of mummy-shaped coffins, lay in a yellow quartzite sarcophagus with a lid of pink granite. This was enclosed in four shrines of gilded wood, set one inside another.

Objects found in the tomb:
1. Ivory headrest
2. Box inlaid with ivory.
3. Alabaster ointment jar in the form of a lion.
4. Drinking cup in the form of a lotus flower.
5. Gold funeral mask inlaid with semi-precious stones.
6. Model of a boat. The Treasury contained a number of these.
7. Gilded wooden figure of Tutankhamun as a harpooner, standing on a papyrus raft.
8. Gold pectoral (chest ornament) set with semi-precious stones. The winged scarab beetle is a symbol of resurrection.
9. Armband with scarab.

New Kingdom tombs were carved out of the hillside itself – in the hope of making them impossible to find, rather than to save expense. But no matter how cunningly the entrances were hidden, robbers found their way in and stole everything of value that they could find.

For many years archaeologists searched for a pharaoh's tomb that still contained its treasure. In 1922 the search was rewarded. In the Valley of the Kings, a royal burial place on the west bank of the Nile, opposite the New Kingdom capital Thebes, the archaeologist Howard Carter found the entrance to the tomb of Tutankhamun. A flight of steps led to a passage filled with rubble, beyond which lay rooms packed with treasure. Though the tomb is more than a thousand years later than the great pyramids of ancient Egypt, it gives some idea of the splendour which must have surrounded the early pharaohs.

GLOSSARY

Amulet A small charm, either worn or carried, which was thought to ward off evil.

Archaeologist A person who learns about the past by unearthing and studying buildings and objects that have survived from former times.

Basalt A very hard, greenish-black or brownish-black rock.

Bitumen A black tar-like mineral.

Bow-drill A drill encircled by the string of a small bow. The bow is pushed back and forth, causing the string to rotate the drill.

Canopic jars Jars used to hold the internal organs of a body. So called because early Egyptologists mistook their figures for representations of the god Osiris, who was worshipped at the city of Canopus in the form of a human-headed jar.

Casing stones The outer stones forming the face of a pyramid.

Causeway A raised path or road made on an embankment.

Chaff Dust made from the outer husks of grain, produced by threshing.

Chase To decorate metal by punching or raising its surface with a tool.

Cult The worship of a particular god.

Delegation A group of people sent to do business on behalf of someone else.

Dolerite A very hard stone, similar to basalt.

Dynasty A succession of rulers belonging to related families. Egypt's pharaohs formed 32 dynasties.

Egyptologist A scholar specialising in the study of ancient Egyptian history.

Embalmer A person whose trade is the preserving of bodies before burial.

Flail A tool consisting of a heavy wooden club, hinged to swing freely from a long handle, which was used to thresh grain.

Flax The plant from which linen is made.

Granite A very hard rock formed mostly of the minerals quartz and feldspar.

Harpoon A lance-like weapon which is thrown to spear fish. A rope is attached to it so that the hunter can haul the fish in.

Hieroglyphs Ancient Egyptian writing. At first picture-signs were used to represent objects. Later the signs came to represent sounds as well.

Horizon The line at which the earth and sky appear to meet.

Hypostyle hall A hall with many pillars.

Ibis A bird related to the heron. The ancient Egyptians believed that it was sacred.

Implement A tool of any kind.

Irrigation The watering of land by artificial means, such as the digging of canals.

Jamb The side-post of a doorway.

Ka One of the aspects of a person's immortal spirit, according to the ancient Egyptians. They believed it was born with a person and accompanied him throughout life like a kind of double. They also believed that if it was given nourishment it would live on after the person's death.

Kingdom A word which, in ancient Egyptian history, means a period of time, not a place. The Old Kingdom includes the Third to Sixth Dynasties (2886–2181 BC), the middle Kingdom the Eleventh to Thirteenth Dynasties (1991–1786 BC), and the New Kingdom the Eighteenth to Twentieth Dynasties (1568–1085 BC).

Limestone A light-coloured rock much used for building as it is plentiful and easily cut.

Lintel A horizontal beam over a doorway or other opening.

Litter A seat or couch mounted on horizontal poles, in which a person could be carried on men's shoulders.

Mastaba An Arabic word meaning 'bench'. The Arabs gave this name to low, flat tombs that reminded them of the shape of a bench.

Mortuary temple A temple associated with the burial of the dead.

Natron A form of soda, found in the ground in various parts of the world.

Oasis A fertile area of land surrounded by desert.

Obelisk A four-sided tapering pillar of stone.

Papyrus A type of reed plentiful in the Nile delta, from which paper can be made.

Patron A person who provides money, or influential support, to help someone to achieve a purpose.

Pectoral An ornament worn on the chest.

Portcullis A heavy door, of stone, metal or wood, which closed by dropping from a recess.

Pylon An Egyptian entrance gate.

Quartzite A rock formed mostly of the mineral quartz.

Quay An artificial landing place built for the unloading of boats.

Regalia the emblems of royalty worn by a king or queen.

Ritual Used in or connected with a religious ceremony.

Sanctuary A special holy place within a temple.

Sarcophagus An outer coffin made of stone.

Scarab A type of beetle.

Scribe A person whose profession is writing on behalf of other people.

Shrine A cupboard-like container in which the image of a god is kept.

Shroud A cloth in which a corpse is wrapped.

Smelt To obtain metal from mineral ore by melting it at a very high temperature.

Stem The curved upright timber at the prow (front) of a boat.

Sternpost A similar timber at the stern (back) of a boat.

Thresh To beat or trample grain crops in order to separate the grain from the husks and straw.

Vizier A ruler's chief minister.

Winnow To use a current of air to blow away chaff during threshing.

INDEX

Page numbers in bold type refer to illustrations.

First published in MCMXCI as *Inside Story – An Egyptian Pyramid* by Macdonald Young Books © The Salariya Book Co Ltd MCMXCI

Look out for these other exciting titles from Book House

World of Wonder

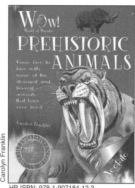

HB ISBN: 978-1-905638-24-6
PB ISBN: 978-1-905638-25-3

HB ISBN: 978-1-907184-04-8
PB ISBN: 978-1-907184-05-5

HB ISBN: 978-1-905638-26-0
PB ISBN: 978-1-905638-27-7

HB ISBN: 978-1-907184-12-3
PB ISBN: 978-1-907184-13-0

HB ISBN: 978-1-906370-16-9
PB ISBN: 978-1-906370-17-6

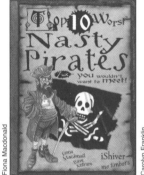

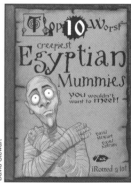

HB ISBN: 978-1-906714-86-4
PB ISBN: 978-1-906714-87-1

HB ISBN: 978-1-907184-46-8
PB ISBN: 978-1-907184-47-5

HB ISBN: 978-1-907184-40-6
PB ISBN: 978-1-907184-41-3

HB ISBN: 978-1-906714-84-0
PB ISBN: 978-1-906714-85-7

HB ISBN: 978-1-907184-44-4
PB ISBN: 978-1-907184-45-1

GRAFFEX

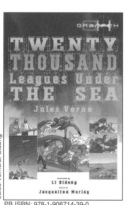

PB ISBN: 978-1-905638-52-9

PB ISBN: 978-1-906714-39-0

PB ISBN: 978-1-906714-73-4

PB ISBN: 978-1-906714-40-6

PB ISBN: 978-1-905638-72-7

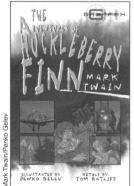
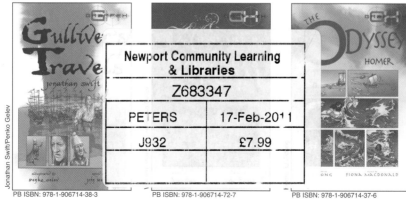
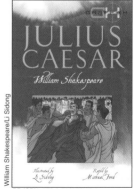

PB ISBN: 978-1-906370-07-7

PB ISBN: 978-1-906714-38-3

PB ISBN: 978-1-906714-72-7

PB ISBN: 978-1-906714-37-6

PB ISBN: 978-1-906370-12-1